S0-BNK-881

William H. Fox Talbot

André Jammes

TR
651
T3413

William H. Fox Talbot

Inventor of the Negative-Positive Process

Macmillan Publishing Co., Inc.

New York

150694

GERTRUDE KISTLER MEMORIAL LIBRARY
ROSEMONT COLLEGE
ROSEMONT, PENNSYLVANIA 19010

TR
651
.T3413
1973

*William H. Fox Talbot: Inventor of the
Negative-Positive Process* is Volume 2 of
PHOTOGRAPHY: MEN AND MOVEMENTS
Edited by Romeo E. Martinez

Copyright © 1972 by
Verlag C. J. Bucher, Luzern und Frankfurt/M
Copyright © 1973 by
Macmillan Publishing Co., Inc.

All rights reserved. No part of this book may be
reproduced or transmitted in any form or by any
means, electronic or mechanical, including
photocopying, recording or by any information
storage and retrieval system, without permission
in writing from the Publisher.

Macmillan Publishing Co., Inc.
866 Third Avenue, New York, N.Y. 10022
Collier-Macmillan Canada Ltd., Toronto, Ontario

Library of Congress Catalog Card Number: 73-10789

First Printing 1973

English translation by Maureen Oberli-Turner
Printed in Switzerland

The Inventors of Photography

Like most other scientific and technical inventions, it is not possible to attribute the invention of photography to a single individual or a single country. France and England produced a number of pioneers simultaneously—accepted and rejected, honored and ignored. It is no easy matter to bring a semblance of order and clarity into this entangled history in which patents, processes, and "open letters" form the basis of the controversy. The first historians of photography were the contemporaries of the pioneers, and their books often read like the speeches of counsels for the defense. They also helped many a tenacious legend to achieve credibility. It was left to modern historians to gather together documents and facts which make it easier for us to judge who really invented what. In his recent well considered and substantial book, Beaumont Newhall was successful in clarifying and evaluating the various contributions, and it has now become clear how the race for recognition, rivalry, and exaggerated claims finally led to the generally accessible knowledge from which modern photography evolved.

Niepce

The real iniator of the medium was indisputably Nicéphore Niepce. As early as 1816, he succeeded in producing images on light-sensitive paper by means of a *camera obscura*, although he was unable to fix them. He made accurate reproductions of lithographs and etchings, he discovered the photogenic quality of Jew's pitch, he invented the iris diaphragm, and he experimented with all the light-sensitive substances known at the time. His extensive correspondence is full of details which prove that he often came extremely close to the "ideal solution." The oldest picture made with the *camera obscura* (between 1826 and 1827), which was rediscovered by Gernsheim, may, by virtue of its simplicity and faintness, be described as a symbolic example of a premature semisuccess, due to the fact that Niepce was born ahead of his time in an era which had not yet learned to organize its scientific knowledge. He lived a secluded life in the province of his birth, far from the centers of intellectual activity. The Napoleonic wars had destroyed all international connections; so he was unable to establish contact with the impulses and movements of the day which helped the English inventor, William H. Fox Talbot, to find his way out of the isolation into which he, too, had voluntarily fled. Niepce's inventive spirit sought access to the new industrial society which developed after the revolution; however, his lack of financial means and adequate technical education caused his downfall, and he died in desperate straits in 1833, leaving to Daguerre (whose partner he had been since 1829) a detailed plan of a developing process—which lacked only the final guiding principle.

Daguerre

Strange how different the characters of these two French inventors were! Niepce: methodical and patient, discreet and reserved, almost suspicious—but all too credulous when it came to making decisions, Daguerre: famous and ambitious; clever—almost too clever—the proud and arrogant miracle worker of the Paris boulevards. His *Diorama* threw the public—who was unable to believe its eyes when confronted with optical illusions endowed with the character of reality—into a frenzy of enthusiasm. But Daguerre, the painter, who succeeded in achieving a previously unattained "veracity"—and who was naturally acquainted with the *camera obscura*—relentlessly pursued the idea of fixing the intangible image. He was neither a scientist nor a researcher, but the passion for his invention bordered on obsession. His wife must have had ample cause for complaint, for he spent days and nights on end repeating Niepce's experiments. More adept than his partner at knocking on the right doors, the free tickets to his *Diorama* shows made attractive gifts to the scientists and optical technicians whose information was so important for his success.

Instead of employing the metal plates which Niepce had used twenty years previously, Daguerre sensitized silver foil with iodine, and with the help of mercury vapor, managed to produce an image. Thus he created—probably in 1835—the first photographic images of any appreciable clarity. Niepce's original experiments had developed into the realization of one of mankind's most cherished dreams: the seizing and fixing of the reflected image.

Daguerre's passionate enthusiasm challenged the doubt in the minds of many scientists. His invention had the impact of a bomb. Arago's interest persuaded the French government and academies to compensate Daguerre, and Niepce's heirs so that the new process could become accessible to the "whole world." On August 19, 1839, the general public was informed of Daguerre's methods, and he was awarded a generous income.

William Henry Fox Talbot: Humanist, Scholar, and Discoverer

At the beginning of 1839, the French press published reports on the projects of Daguerre and Arago. The details of the process remained secret, but the innovation itself was received with astonishment and enthusiasm all over the world. In England, the news aroused the particular interest of a man called William Henry Fox Talbot, a member of the Royal Society, and a man who had set his sights for the same goal as Daguerre and whose achievements were of great importance.

Fox Talbot was born in February 1800, and his family can be traced back to the fifteenth century. He was owner of an enviable country seat near Bath called Lacock Abbey

—today under the care of the National Trust. The Abbey library, the greater part of which Talbot himself assembled, documents the wide range of his interests and is now open to the public. Talbot took a number of pictures of this "shrine," and the photograph dating from 1844, entitled "A Scene in a Library," reveals much about his interests: *The Philosophical Magazine, Manners and Customs of the Ancient Egyptians, Philological Essays, Miscellanies of Science, Storia pittorica dell'Italia* by Luigi Lanzi, botanical journals, etc. His intellectual interests were extremely varied and ranged from natural science to ancient history, linguistics to the fine arts. At the age of twenty-two he wrote a memorandum on the properties of a "curve described by a symmetrical hyperbola." *The Philosophical Magazine,* the *Quarterly Journal of Science,* and the *Edinburgh Journal of Science* published essays which bear witness to his knowledge of the physical laws of light: treatises on experiments with colored flames, on chromatic light and intense homogenous light, and on the nature of light itself.

In addition, Talbot made a translation of *Macbeth* into Greek verse—an achievement which proves him to have been a first-class humanist. He was familiar with Hebrew script and was able to decipher Babylonian cuneiform inscriptions; he studied and photographed hieroglyphics, and he was the author of an Assyrian dictionary.

At the age of thirty-three he was elected a member of the Royal Society—no small honor! In addition, Fox Talbot was active in a number of scientific committees.

This proud rival of the French pioneers entered the battle, liberally equipped with decorations of honor and impressive titles. He was totally unimpressed by the discoveries of "Arago's protégé," whom he regarded as a mere buffoon. Fox Talbot's lack of sociability and arrogance increased at the same rate as Daguerre's popularity.

The Birth of an Idea

Niepce's pursuit of his invention was based largely on his urge to reproduce lithographs as accurately as possible; Daguerre's subsequent development of Niepce's experiments was motivated by his desire to endow the "optical illusions" of his *Diorama* shows with an element of reality. Talbot, on the other hand, was interested in the permanent conservation of images of the Italian countryside, which he had succeeded in reproducing as paper prints, with the help of the *camera obscura.* From the very beginning, his pioneer work was artistic in nature, and at the same time, clearly directed toward his final aim: the unlimited reproduction of the image, its realism, and its documentary value.

"One of the first days of the month of October 1833, I was amusing myself on the lovely shores of Lake Como, in Italy, taking sketches with Wollaston's *camera lucida.* In honesty, I should say, attempting to take them, but with the smallest possible amount of success. For when the eye was removed from the prism, in which all looked beautiful,

I found that the faithless pencil had left only traces on the paper melancholy to behold. I then thought of trying again a method which I had tried many years before. This method was to take a *camera obscura* and to throw the image of the objects on a piece of transparent tracing paper laid on a pane of glass in the focus of the instrument. This led me to reflect on the inimitable beauty of the pictures of nature's painting, which the glass lens of the camera throws upon the paper in its focus—fairy pictures, creations of a moment, and destined as rapidly to fade away. It was during these thoughts that the idea occurred to me: how charming it would be if it were possible to cause these natural images to imprint themselves durably and remain fixed upon the paper! And why should it not be possible? I asked myself."

Silver Nitrate

After an extended tour of Europe (he was passionately fond of traveling), Talbot returned to England in January 1834 and began experiments aimed at realizing his dreams and speculations. It was natural enough that he should use the well-known properties of silver nitrate, a white substance which turned black when exposed to light. He applied a silver nitrate solution to paper, by means of a paintbrush, and inserted the sheet of paper in the *camera obscura.* But the image developed very slowly. Similar experiments with a silver chloride solution were no more successful. Talbot had progressed no further than his predecessors.

Silver Chloride

Talbot now hit upon the idea of using silver chloride at the moment of its formation on the paper itself. He did this by dipping the paper in a saltwater solution, allowing it to dry, and subsequently painting it with silver nitrate. The chemical reaction between the two substances resulted in a precipitation of silver chloride. Talbot experimented with various amounts of salt and discovered that a weak solution produced a much more light-sensitive substance. This was a remarkable milestone, compared to the earlier achievements of Wedgwood and Davy. Talbot had succeeded in producing an image in the *camera obscura!*

Relative Durability of the Image

The second important step was Talbot's recognition of the possibilities offered by the meager sensitivity of silver chloride, combined with an excess of nitrate (in the salt), in the stabilization of the image. By dipping the picture in a solution of boiling salt water, he was able to make the silver salts relatively insensitive, although he had not yet succeeded in "fixing" the image. (Many of Talbot's experiments during this period have been preserved.)

The First Photogrammes

The invention was not yet complete, but Talbot was now

able to obtain "distinct and very pleasing images of such things as leaves, lace, and other flat objects with complicated forms and outlines, by exposing them to the light of the sun." He achieved these images—which were contact prints in the truest sense of the word—by placing the object directly on the sensitized paper, weighting it with a glass plate, and exposing it to sunlight. The old technique of *typographia naturalis*, known to printers since the time of Leonardo da Vinci, was reborn through Talbot. A facsimile of Talbot's handwriting "copied" by this method, and dated June 20, 1835, has been published by Eugen Ostroff.

First Experiments with the Camera Obscura

The difficulty of producing a satisfactory picture in the *camera obscura* remained. ". . . when the sensitive paper was placed in the focus of a *camera obscura* and directed at any object, a building, for instance, during a moderate space of time, such as an hour or two, the effect produced upon the paper was not strong enough to exhibit as satisfactory a picture of the building as had been hoped for. The outline of the roof and of the chimneys, etc., against the sky was marked enough, but the details of the architecture were feeble, and the parts in shade were left either blank or nearly so."

Talbot then developed the idea of concentrating the light rays onto a small area but using a very small camera case and a short focal length—a contraption to which his wife somewhat disrespectfully referred as a "mousetrap." "During the brilliant summer of 1835 in England, I made new attempts to obtain pictures of buildings with the *camera obscura*. Having devised a process which gave additional sensibility to the paper, by giving it repeated alternate washes of salt and silver and using it in a moist state, I succeeded in reducing the time necessary for obtaining an image with the *camera obscura* on a bright day . . . to ten minutes. But these pictures, though very pretty, were very small and comparatively miniature."

The First Negative

The Science Museum in London possesses a negative image on paper, of a casement window in Lacock Abbey, measuring approximately one square inch. The picture was taken from inside, and every small pane of glass set in lead is clearly delineated. This is the oldest known negative in existence, and it bears the following handwritten inscription: "Latticed Window, (with the *camera obscura*) August 1835. When first made, the squares of glass, about 200 in number, could be counted with the help of a glass."

Micrography

In the same summer of 1835, which had begun so well for Talbot, he resumed work on Davy's experiments with the solar microscope and achieved some remarkable images on paper. "When a sheet of this, which I shall call 'Sensitive Paper,' is placed in a dark chamber, and the magnified image of some object is thrown on it by the solar microscope, after the lapse of perhaps a quarter of an hour, the picture is completed. I have not as yet used high magnifying powers, on account of the consequent enfeeblement of the light. Of course, with a more sensitive paper, greater magnifying power will become possible. On examining one of these pictures, which I made about three and a half years ago [this was written in January 1839], I find, by actual measurement of the picture and the object, that the latter is magnified seventeen times in linear diameter, and consequently, in surface 289 times. I have others which I believe are considerably more magnified, but I have lost the corresponding objects; so I cannot here state the exact number."

The Science Museum in London possesses a number of these microphotographs.

A Harsh Awakening

After Talbot had investigated the essential problems of photography and had recognized the fact that the perfection of his discoveries required more time than he had at his disposal, he abandoned this aspect of his work. "During the three following years not much was added to previous knowledge. Want of sufficient leisure for experiments was a great obstacle and hindrance, and I almost resolved to publish some account of the art in the imperfect state in which it then was." Talbot's scientific work left him no time for experiments in the photographic field. He began work on a synthesis of his archeological and philological knowledge, an austere work entitled *Hermes or Classical and Antiquarian Research*.

Talbot states frankly that he had abandoned his experiment—for the time being at any rate. He repeats in *The Pencil of Nature*: "However curious the results which I had met with, I still felt convinced that much more important things must remain behind, and that the clue was still wanting to the labyrinth of facts. But as there seemed no immediate prospect of further success, I thought of drawing up a short account of what had been done, and presenting it to the Royal Society."

There seemed to be no need for hurry, and his first discoveries might well have remained buried in their early stages had not the hullabaloo over Daguerre, on the other side of the Channel, aroused his ambition and spurred him on to fresh activity. (This was one of the French inventor's indirect services to photography!) Talbot was suddenly confronted by the classical dilemma of the inventor: "An event occurred in the scientific world, which in some degree frustrated the hope with which I had for five years pursued this long and complicated but interesting series of experiments—namely, the hope of being the first to announce to the world the existence of the new art, which has since been named photography. I allude, of course, to the publication

7

in the month of January 1839, of the great discovery of M. Daguerre, of the photographic process which he has called the Daguerreotype. I need not speak of the sensation created in all parts of the world by the first announcement of this splendid discovery, or rather, of the fact of its having been made (for the actual method used was kept secret for many months longer). This great and sudden fame had two causes: first, the beauty of the discovery itself; second, the zealous enthusiasm of Arago, whose eloquence was inspired by personal friendship. He extolled the inventor of this new art, sometimes to the assembled staff of the French Academy and at other times to the less scientific judgment, but no less eager patriotism, of the Chamber of Deputies. . . ."

Talbot Publishes His Work

Talbot did not have a moment to lose. The French government, urged on by Arago, was on the point of purchasing and publishing Daguerre's process. It was therefore extremely important for Talbot to publish the results which he had achieved. So as not to fall behind, Talbot wrote to Arago and Biot regarding the fixing of *camera obscura* images and the possibility of preserving these images, even when they were exposed to sunlight. A lively exchange of letters developed (in French) between Biot and Talbot (a critical edition of which would be of great value).

Talbot's first step was to send his correspondents some examples of his "photogenic drawings," a number of which were exhibited on January 25 by Faraday, the secretary of the Royal Institution, in the Institution's library. The public was able to compare Talbot's work with the rival French invention, and the achievements of the "genius Talbot" were greatly admired: "Flowers and leaves; a pattern of lace; figures taken from painted glass; a view of Venice, copied from an engraving; some images formed by the solar microscope, namely a very highly magnified slice of wood, exhibiting pores of two kinds—one set much smaller than the other, and more numerous; another microscopic sketch exhibiting the reticulation of the wing of an insect; finally, various pictures, representing the architecture of my house in the country, all made in the summer of 1835 wiht the *camera obscura*. I believe this to be the first instance on record of a house having painted its own portrait." (Talbot was unaware of a similar attempt by Niepce made between 1826 and 1827.) "You make the powers of nature work for you!" exclaimed Talbot enthusiastically, "No human hand has hitherto traced such lines as these drawings display." The famous Faraday, who presented his exhibition, proclaimed: "What man may hereafter do, now that Dame Nature has become his drawing mistress, is impossible to predict." And Gernsheim draws attention to the fact that among the exhibited "photogenic drawings" were reproductions of etchings made "by first getting them with the lights and shades reversed and then copying from

the reversed impression"—a description which amounts to the definition of a negative and its use for the productions of positive prints. This simple but nevertheless brilliant idea, which had not occurred to either Niepce or Bayard, dates from before 1839; it is also certain that the views of Lacock Abbey exhibited by Faraday were positive images.

Some Account . . .

On January 31, 1839, Talbot once again presented the Royal Society with specimens of his work, accompanied by his own comments on his process which he had written with the greatest care and concentration over a period of several weeks. This work was entitled "Some account of the art of photogenic drawing, or the process by which natural objects may be made to delineate themselves without the aid of the artist's pencil." Talbot reprinted this memorandum as a fourteen-page pamphlet for private distribution; in this form (according to Beaumont Newhall) it is the first separate publication on photography in the world. In it Talbot reports on the origins, successes, and failures of the new medium and makes some interesting prognoses concerning its future.

The Photographic Image

Talbot also clearly defined the formation of the image: "The light acting on the paper would naturally blacken it, while the parts in shadow would retain their whiteness. Thus I expected that a kind of image or picture would be produced, resembling to a certain degree the object from which it was derived."

Talbot deliberately avoided including details of the substances used, while at the same time praising their revolutionary success: "Indeed, such is the speed of the effect produced, that the picture may be said to be ended almost as soon as it is begun. To give some more definite idea of the rapidity of the process, I will state, that after various trials the nearest evaluation which I could make of the time necessary for obtaining the picture of an object, so to have pretty distinct outlines, when I employed the full sunshine, was *half a second*." He also developed a theory concerning the stabilization of the image: "The nitrate of silver, which has become black by the action of light, is no longer the same chemical substance that it was before. Consequently, if a picture produced by solar light is subjected afterward to any chemical process, the white and dark parts of it will be differently acted upon; and there is no evidence that after this action has taken place, these white and dark parts will any longer be subject to a spontaneous change. . . . This chemical change, which I call the *preserving process*, is far more effectual than could have been anticipated. The paper, which had previously been so sensitive to light, becomes completely insensitive to it, to such a degree that I am able to show the Society specimens which have been exposed for an hour to the full summer sun. . . ."

The Negative

The immense value of this technical innovation is succinctly indicated in the following formulation: "If the picture so obtained is first *preserved* so as to bear sunshine, it may be afterward employed as an object to be copied, and by means of this second process, the lights and shadows are brought back to their original dispositive."

Prints from Nature

Talbot evidently preferred to draw the attention of his readers to the possible uses of his process rather than to provide them with information about the exact techniques and procedures employed. First of all, he indicated the advantages of images produced by contact with flat objects (plants, lace, etc.). He then went on to discuss the most difficult problem—that of the portrait, whereby he spoke only of the possibility of creating shadow-pictures, the most transitory of things—the proverbial symbol of all that is fleeting and momentary. But the silhouettes, he stated, possessed the advantage of accuracy.

"The hand is liable to err from the true outline, and a very small deviation causes a notable diminution in the resemblance. I believe this manual process cannot be compared with the truth and fidelity which the portrait is given by means of solar light." Talbot also mentions a further possibility of photogenic drawing: the reproduction of paintings on glass. The process was based on contact copies of drawings or paintings on glass or sensitized paper—a method which was later to become famous when Corot reintroduced it, in collaboration with some photographer friends, under the name of *cliché verre* (glass negative).

Microphotography

The use of the microscope, as proposed by Talbot in his memorandum, without doubt represents one of the most important aspects of the new process, and there are some remarkable examples still in existence. Talbot was successful in producing images that were far more accurate than the most skilled draftsman could have created, and in a far shorter period of time: in short, in producing images capable of capturing fleeting phenomena: "This process not only saves us time and trouble, but there are many objects—especially microscopic crystallizations—that alter so greatly in the course of three or four days (and it could hardly take any artist less to delineate them in all their details), that they could never be drawn in the usual way."

The Image in the Camera

By far the most interesting passage in Talbot's memorandum to the Royal Society concerned the image produced in the camera: "The most curious application of this art... the most surprising to those who have examined my collection!" Talbot writes with great enthusiasm and emotion of "the beautiful effects which are produced by a *camera*

obscura... the vivid picture of external nature which it displays... the lovely scene which thus illuminates it for a moment...." Unfortunately, this aspect of his art was insufficiently developed, and he was only able to produce tiny images or architectural pictures in which the areas in shadow did not appear on the paper.

Facsimiles

The final aspect of the art of "photogenic drawing" was the reproduction of etchings and prints in a transparent process. This form of contact print has, however, been developed to such a degree since Talbot's early experiments—even though it is only possible to employ it for originals printed on one side of the paper—that there is no point in pursuing the immense significance of this aspect of Talbot's technique.

Talbot and the French Academicians

Talbot's memorandum, dated January 31, 1839, was written in haste and is in many ways confusing. Conceived as a collection of technical, aesthetic, and practical deliberations, it contains a great many gaps and omissions. Biot drew Talbot's attention to this fact in a tactful letter: "...it is regrettable that the text contains no special reference to the production of the 'sensitive paper.'" He remarked that a publication available to the general public would be of great value to the experimenters. In order to anticipate the possibility of a publication by Daguerre (who had without hesitation secretly resumed work on Niepce's experiments with images on paper), Talbot appealed to Biot in two consecutive letters, written in French. He precisely defined the production of his sensitized paper by means of silver chloride and a precipitation of nitrate and explained the first method of treatment with potassium iodide which rendered the image partially insensitive. He also drew attention to a second process which gave the image a relatively high durability, for which he used a concentrated sea-salt solution. In his letter of March 1, Talbot wrote: "The third method of fixing a photogenic drawing is based on the use of ferrocyanide of potassium." Finally he admitted with candor the valuable influence which John F. W. Herschel's contribution had had on his invention: "The fourth process (which is worth more than all the others put together), is based on bathing the image in sodium hyposulphite.* Herschel must have stumbled upon this

---

* The prefix "hypo" has traditionally been used by chemists to indicate a lower state of oxidation. Herschel named the acid, $H_2S_2O_3$, "hyposulphurous," because he thought that in its oxygen-sulphur ratio it was next lower to sulphurous acid. However, in 1861, the French chemist, P. Schützenberger, discovered the acid $H_2S_2O_4$. It occupies the very position Herschel assigned to his acid; so a change in nomenclature became necessary. Herschel's acid, now called thiosulphuric, became $H_2S_2O_3 \rightarrow H_2O = S_2O_2$ (Beaumont Newhall). Today we recognize "hypo" to have the formula $Na_2S_2O_3 = 5 H_2O$, and its name has been changed to "sodium thiosulphate."

process almost by chance, since it was he who discovered 'acide hyposulfureux' and its essential characteristics, including the ability of sodium hyposulphite to dissolve silver chloride (a substance usually hard to dissolve). This property had not previously been used, but there is no doubt that it will be widely used in future. . . . The technique of retaining the image, i.e., of fixing, is basically different from the other three processes, since the silver salts are not fixed or rendered insensitive in the white sections of the image but removed entirely."

Thanks to Herschel's genius, Talbot now had at his disposal a complete photographic process which covered both the sensitization and the fixing of the picture. Unfortunately, however, he refused to collaborate with this famous chemist and astronomer—a collaboration which would without doubt have led to a spectacularly rapid development in the photographic field. When it came to Herschel's attention that Daguerre had achieved the fixing of the image in the *camera obscura,* he shut himself up in his laboratory for days on end, and by the end of January he had made all the discoveries which had taken Talbot five years. Herschel informed Talbot of the results of his investigations but received no reply; he was generous enough to keep his discoveries a secret so that his colleague might reap the benefit of his research.

The chemical powers of sodium thiosulphate thus first became known in France through Biot's publication of Talbot's letter, and Daguerre immediately began working with the chemical. In his letter dated March 1, 1839, Talbot also wrote of a new process of sensitization by means of silver bromide: "At four o'clock in the afternoon, with a clouded, grey sky over London, it took only seven minutes to form the image of a window in the *camera obscura.*"

Daguerre's Triumph

During this period, Arago found himself in a difficult situation. He was well aware that Daguerre's invention was in a dangerous position, and that it was necessary to take speedy action if the official initiative were not to be lost for the support of an invention which was no longer new. Arago therefore presented a project on June 15, which he himself defended and which, with his emphatic support, was accepted by the Chamber of Deputies on July 3; Gay-Lussac recommended it to the Senate on July 17. Daguerre received an income of 6000 francs and Isidore Niepce an income of 4000 francs. On August 19, at a solemn meeting of the *Académie des Sciences* and the *Académie des Beaux-Arts,* Arago made Daguerre's secret public. The enthusiasm in both the scientific and artistic worlds knew no bounds, but the public reserved its opinion until the theory became practice and it was possible to admire the achievements of both masters and pupils.

The Daguerreotype and its English Admirers

English scholars did not wait for the official consecration of August 19 to gather information about the remarkable qualities of the Daguerreotype. Numerous members of the Royal Society accepted an invitation from Arago to travel to Paris, and their astonishment and admiration were unlimited. Herschel's reports to Talbot on the quality of Daguerre's plates contain so many superlatives that the English inventor must have reacted with a certain resentment and bitterness. "It is hardly saying too much to call them miraculous," wrote Herschel. "Certainly they surpass anything I could have conceived as within the bounds of reasonable expectation. The most elaborate engraving falls far short of the richness and delicateness of execution, every gradation of light and shade is given with a softness and fidelity which sets all painting at an immeasurable distance. His *times* are also very short. In a bright day three minutes suffice. In short, if you have a few days at your disposition, I cannot commend you better than to *come and see.* Excuse this ebullition!" Beaumont Newhall quotes this text, and those of other eminent English scholars, including James David Forbes: "I have no hesitation in saying I was pleased beyond my most sanguine expectations . . . in short, it baffles belief." Sir John Robison wrote: ". . . in truth, the distinctness, and fidelity of the minutest details were so exquisite, that color could have added little to the charm felt in contemplating them. . . ."

After his return to England, Herschel carefully reconsidered the problems, advantages and disadvantages of the Daguerreotype as opposed to those of the process using paper, and his letter dated June 24 evidently contributed to Talbot's renewed vigor in this unequal battle: "When I wrote you from Paris I was just warm from the impression of Daguerre's wonderful pictures. After reflection, I feel in no way disposed to abate my admiration. However, that has not prevented my wishing that the processes which have paper for their field of display should be perfected, as I do not see how else the multiplication of copies can take place, a branch of the photographic art which Daguerre's processes do not by his own account admit of."

The Latent Image

Talbot's courage did not fail him in the solitude of his laboratory. Convinced of the superiority of his methods, he now pressed forward to perfect his methods using paper. He made little progress, however, for it proved difficult to shorten the exposures of the paper by direct blackening of the light-sensitive emulsion. The correspondence between Talbot and Biot came to a standstill. Then, on January 18, 1841, Talbot wrote a letter which reads like a shout of triumph: ". . . last September I discovered a means of greatly increasing the sensibility of the light-sensitive paper; it is no less than one hundred times greater. . . ." On February 1 he wrote in greater detail: "I lay a sheet of paper in the camera, remove it after a few moments, study it carefully and cannot establish the faintest hint of an image. The picture is nevertheless there in absolute perfection, but absolutely invisible.... I shall show you how I can make the image appear in a perfectly simple manner as if by magic. This is really the most wonderful thing you can possibly imagine; the first time it happened I was truly dumbfounded."

Talbot had discovered the development of the latent image; as the imaginative Herschel was to say later—"the awakening of the sleeping picture." This was a decisive moment in the history of photography. "I consider the leading feature in the said invention to have been the discovery of the existence of invisible photographic images upon paper, and the mode of making them visible ... and I say that such an invention was a new one to the best of my judgement and belief, and that it was of great importance in photography, and that it has continued to be used by photographers ever since the time of its publication" (J. F. W. Herschel, May 25, 1854).

Only Daguerre had experienced something similar, when mercury vapor suddenly and unexpectedly conjured up an image on the virgin silver plate. But this first coincidence cannot really be compared to the second, since the chemical processes involved are totally different, and it was only Talbot's method which proved capable of development.

Six month after Daguerre's triumph, Talbot found himself in the strange position of a scientist who, although he had developed an excellent and extremely promising technique, had nevertheless found neither recognition nor the possibility of utilizing his invention. His rival had succeeded in showing the public some immediate results—even if they were on a restricted scale. Talbot was convinced that the Daguerreotype had no future, and he was thoroughly aware of the almost inexhaustible possibilities of his own process, but he did not enjoy even a fraction of the fame which surrounded Daguerre. Thus the generosity of this Englishman—who had, after all, informed the French academicians of his methods and published the basic essentials of his process—turned to mistrust. He surrounded himself with patents. That which he had previously given freely to the public for sake of a vestige of fame, he now took pains to protect with all the legal means at his disposal —almost to the point of meanness. Talbot, who had once refused to accept the advice of the famous David Brewster: "I do not see why a gentleman with an independent fortune should scruple to accept of any benefit that he derived from his own genius," was now entirely in accord with this attitude. On February 8, 1841, he applied for the patent of his "Calotype Photographic Process," the specifications for which were deposited on July 29 and registered on August 17. The new word "calotype" (from the Greek *kalos,* meaning beautiful, magnificent), covered the entire process. In a shortened form, the patent specification read as follows: "I claim to be the originator firstly: of the use of gallic acid or a solution of the same, combined with a silver solution in order to render specially prepared paper more sensitive to light; secondly: of the methods by which images are made visible (or clearer, should they be too weak) on paper,

by treating them with liquids on the sections already influenced by the action of light; thirdly: for the creation of portraits of living subjects by photographic means on paper; fourthly: of the use of potassium bromide or any other bromide solution for the fixing of the image obtained" (from the *Bulletin de la Société française de photographie,* July 1857). Talbot's communication appeared in the *Proceedings* of the Royal Society, and he also had a limited number of copies printed privately. This text, dated June 10, 1841, marks an important point in the history of photography, since it contains elements which were to open up wider horizons than those of the Daguerreotype.

Attempts at Exploitation

Basically, this report consisted of the same text as that of the patent specifications, but it was more detailed. Talbot was familiar enough with the regulations of the patent office, for he had wanted to patent an invention some time previously—an internal-combustion engine for a mixture of oxygen and hydrogen (shades of Claude and Nicéphore Niepce and their "pyrélophore"!). It is important, however, to draw attention to some discrepancies in the official text: Why, for example, did Talbot not patent the use of the negative in the production of positive prints, since this invention was entirely and indisputably his own? And why did he patent the production of portraits, when, according to English law, it is only the technique used which is of importance? And what led him to include the use of potassium iodide in the fixing of the pictures, when he had emphasized since March 1839 that sodium thiosulphate was preferable? There is no doubt that he had certain scruples about patenting a process which had been suggested to him by his friend Herschel—an opponent of all patents. But his scruples were short-lived, as we shall see. In any case, Talbot had no inhibitions about patenting Joseph Bancroft Reade's idea of the use of gallic acid.

It was now essential that Talbot should tenaciously pursue the possibilities of the exploitation of his process in order to ensure its exclusiveness, and to this end, he promoted an employee, who had been occupied as a laboratory worker, to the head of an establishment situated halfway between London and Lacock Abbey.

The employee, Nicolaas Henneman, managed this first small factory from the autumn of 1843, secured the entire development of photographic production, and brought a large number of photographs onto the market under the name of "Talbotype Photogenic Drawings. Patent."

In embarking on this propagation of his images, Talbot was less concerned with any immediate financial gain than with arousing the attention of photographers interested in acquiring a license from the inventor—a costly affair. His success was only moderate, but it resulted in the creation of the remarkable publication entitled *The Pencil of Nature.*

This work, which consists of pictures and captions, was probably the first publication to reveal the alliance between two techniques—an alliance which provided the development of printing technique with a tremendous impetus and may be regarded as one of the most important volumes of its kind since Gutenberg. *The Pencil of Nature* consists of eighty pages in quarto format, with twenty-four mounted photographic images, preceded by some "introductory remarks" and a short history of the calotype, entitled "Brief Historical Sketch of the Invention of the Art." The work appeared in installments, as was usual for expensive art books in the nineteenth century. The first installment appeared in May or the beginning of June 1844; the sixth and last in April 1846. Each image was accompanied by a commentary, and the pictures (more or less faded in the few copies still in existence) are well worth careful study, especially in connection with Talbot's footnotes. Our modern eyes have become so used to the photographic image that we find it difficult to imagine the astonishment and incredulity of the first subscribers to *The Pencil of Nature*. The pasted-in note which accompanied the first installment reads as follows: "Notice to the reader. The plates of the present work are impressed by the agency of light alone, without any aid whatever from the artist's pencil. They are the sun-pictures themselves, and not, as some persons have imagined, engravings in imitation."

City views, monuments, architectural details, sculptures, artistic documents, still lifes, botanic images, facsimiles of books and etchings, genre pictures—on each of these subjects Talbot made a remarkably shrewd commentary. With his alert eye and his enthusiastic spirit, he endowed all his pictures with the new, specific quality of the photographic art which distinguished it from the previously known reproduction techniques.

With his very first picture (Queen's College, Oxford), Talbot drew attention to the specific characteristics of the new medium, and its ability to capture ". . the most evident marks of the injuries of time . . the abraded state of the stone. . . ." He noted the abundance of detail in a view of Paris: "A single shutter standing open projects far enough forward to catch a gleam of sunshine. . . ." He recognized the immense possibilities of photography for recording works of art and for use in legal proceedings: ". . . should a thief afterwards purloin the treasure . . it would be evidence of a novel kind. . . " He was particularly interested in the two-dimensional reproduction of sculpture and remarked on the extraordinary variety of images obtainable by the use of different lighting conditions and camera standpoints. He advocated the use of the contact print for scientific purposes—above all for the reproduction of herbaria—and predicted the future of microfilm and the photostat. (As an example, he included a page of one of Caxton's incunabula.) He was also interested in the reproduction of etchings, and he was evidently particularly fascinated by the selection and enlargement of detail in an etching. As for the purely artistic point of view, most of his subjects were in the style of the "old Dutchmen": a broom in a half-open door, or a ladder leaning against a haystack. He also showed that his way of seeing was new: ". . . a painter's eye will often be arrested where ordinary people see nothing remarkable . . . a casual gleam of sunshine, or a shadow thrown across his path. . . ."

One of the plates is entitled "A scene in a library." The selection of the books shown is evidently planned and bears witness to the wide range of his intellectual interests; the accompanying text reveals his lively imagination. In his capacity as scientist, he sets forth the photographic possibilities of capturing rays, which, although invisible to the human eye, nevertheless exist outside the visible spectrum. He imagines a dark room penetrated only by these rays and states that it should be possible to take a picture of a person in this darkness: ". . . what a *dénouement* we should have, if we could suppose the secrets of the darkened chamber to be revealed by the testimony of the imprinted paper!" These are truly prophetic words which foresee infrared photography.

The first installment of *The Pencil of Nature* appeared in an edition of approximately two hundred copies, but the number of subscribers dwindled in the course of publication due to the high price, the delay in delivery, and the instability of the pictures. Parallel to *The Pencil of Nature*, Talbot published a collection of photographs of views of Scotland, made famous by the writings of Sir Walter Scott. *Sun Pictures in Scotland* appeared in the autumn of 1845, prior to the publication of the final installment of *The Pencil of Nature*, and consisted of twenty-three pictures without accompanying text. The fact that this collection appeared before the completion of *The Pencil of Nature* gives rise to the supposition that Talbot felt it necessary to try and improve his reputation, which had suffered due to the lack of stability of the *Pencil* prints. The circulation of these Scottish views was smaller than that of *The Pencil of Nature*, but nevertheless remakable for such a primitive studio.

Another production by the Reading Studio was recently discovered by the late Dr. Schültze and was entitled *Record of the Death Bed of C. M. W.* Published shortly before *The Pencil of Nature*, it contained a photographic reproduction of a portrait of Catherine M. Walter and was not available to the general public. Although this publication aroused little interest, it is nevertheless of historical importance, since it represents the first example of photographic illustration. Following the publication of *The Pencil of Nature*, the productivity of the Reading Studio (originally a derelict school), where Henneman worked, increased considerably. Talbot had engaged Thomas A. Malone, who was later to become famous, and these men, working in secret (and incidentally, suspected of producing forged money), achieved some remarkable results. Apart from the three works already mentioned, they produced thousands of prints, some of which appeared in the June 1, 1846 issue of *The Art Union*. Also worthy of mention are the sixty-six illustrations in the fourth volume of *Annals of the Artists of Spain* by William Stirling, only twenty-five of which were published, and which represents the first book on art to be illustrated by photographs. In his outstanding book, *Prints and Visual Communication*, William Ivins drew attention to the importance of this work with the words: "Because of its method of illustration it is to be regarded as the cornerstone of all modern artistic connoisseurship; it contained the first exactly repeatable pictorial statements about works of art which could be accepted as visual evidence about things other than mere iconography. It was no longer necessary to put faith in the accuracy of the observation and skill of the draftsmen and the engravers. These reports were not only impersonal, but they revealed the personality of the artists who made the objects that were reproduced."

The Expansion of the Calotype

Talbot's incontestable success was, at least in his eyes, not nearly as great as the constantly increasing popularity of the Daguerre process. The reason for this was that the Daguerreotype quickly proved to be admirably suited to portraiture. The exceptionally sharp contours produced on the silver plates and the relatively short exposure length proved extremely profitable to a great number of artists all over the world. Talbot was confronted with this new, popular, and lucrative activity even in England (where Daguerre had patented his process).

In 1847, Henneman and Malone opened a studio in Regent Street for the purpose of producing portraits by the calotype process which were artistically superior to the Daguerre portraits. Although the establishment enjoyed the patronage of Queen Victoria, its success was only moderate, and investigations carried out by Harold White and Gernsheim reveal that the two partners received only forty-seven orders over a period of four months.

The uncertainty of the situation regarding photography in England discouraged a considerable number of photographers who otherwise might have contributed to the development of the medium. This was not the case in Scotland, however, for that country enjoyed a legal independence which made it possible to ignore Talbot's patent. Since the paper process had become known, Scottish artists and scientists had made use of it with considerable skill and intrepidity, as for example David Brewster, John Adamson, David Octavius Hill, and Thomas Keith. Success in England would probably have been far greater if the inventor of the new art had not imposed artifical restrictions upon it.

France also benefitted indirectly from the calotype process. After the first ten years, the frenzy of enthusiasm for the Daguerreotype died down, and the best photographers and numerous painters turned to "photogenic paper," the advantages of which had been revealed by experiments of Bayard and Blanquart-Evrard. Following the first tentative attempts of the 1840s, a sudden breakthrough occurred, and Le Gray, Baldus, and Le Secq succeeded in producing genuine works of art. Thus the calotype, technically greatly improved, reached its full development in France.

The Photomechanical Process

One of the weaknesses of Talbot's invention lay in the instability of the paper image for which, in the early stages, a really efficient method of fixing had not been developed. In addition, the copying process by hand was both slow and costly. Talbot, therefore, looked for a way of using the gravure printing process in photography—a procedure upon which both Niepce and the illustrious Fizeau had already embarked. The former made use of the chemical properties of Jew's pitch, whereas Fizeau engraved directly on the Daguerre plate. It was Talbot who first discovered the properties of potassium bichromate (already indicated by Ponton in 1839) and used it for the engraving of metal plates. By this means it was possible for him to overcome the enormous difficulties connected with the reproduction of halftones.

Talbot covered his steel plates with a layer of potassium bichromate dissolved in gelatin, a substance which was insoluble in water once it had been exposed to sunlight. Thus it was only necessary to lay an object or a negative on a plate treated in this way (resulting in a contact print) and expose and wash the plate. This washing removed the chromium salts and the greater part of the gelatin on the uncovered areas. Talbot then immersed the metal in an acid bath which corroded the sensitive areas without altering the sections hardened by gelatin. Thus the plate was transformed into something of a photographic etching. The actual print was made by the usual method of spreading ink on the plate and placing sheets of paper between two impression cylinders. Talbot patented this process on October 29, 1852.

Talbot's description of this procedure reveals that he had succeeded in obtaining only "corroded" and "protected" areas on the plate, i.e., black sections, where the ink was retained, and white areas on the smooth, uncorroded sections. He was, in fact, using traditional techniques in a new way. By powdering the dried gelatin with resin dust, he was able to dissolve the surface into innumerable points (or dots), and a warming of the plate resulted in the resin dust melting and leaving minute spaces. The next chemical employed, ferric chloride, "burnt" numerous tiny holes in the surface of the metal in proportion to the hardness of the gelatin surface. By using the old etching process for the new medium of photography, Talbot created an exact and uncomplicated procedure known as *photoglyphy*, which he patented in 1858. What was lacking in Talbot's work was a rational method for screening the surface to be photographed. Recent research in Lacock Abbey has revealed that the English inventor had already conceived the idea of placing various "screening" devices between the negative and the plate—a very finely woven tissue of 45 percent meshes and paper with lines of various angles produced by a special machine, or the natural markings of cartilaginous leaves. Many of these experiments date back to 1852, and future research will show that Talbot adopted a number of the discoveries of his contemporaries in order to develop them in the most advantageous manner.

Bitterness and Conflict

Genius and conceit were equally strong components of Talbot's character. We have already seen that he tended to regard himself as the one and only inventor of photography and rejected the claims of other researchers. He considered the Daguerreotype to be no more than a mere coincidence and of little value. The only thing which counted was the paper print, positive or negative. His conviction as to the value of his invention was doubtless justified, but after the appearance of the collodion process he did not hesitate to state during a famous legal proceeding: "I consider the said collodion process to be only a variation."

When Blanquart-Evrard published his improved process of printing photographs on paper in 1847—in which he omitted to mention the work of other inventors when presenting his concept to the Academy of Science—Talbot was unable to contain himself and flatly refused to concede any value to the improvement in the process which this "amateur from Lille," as he called Blanquart-Evrard, had achieved. Notes written in French, discovered after his death, state: "What a strange mistake for Mr. Blanquart-Evrard to make! He actually regards himself as the inventor of *my* invention—a hallucination unprecedented in the history of science." By means of concealed falsehoods in his patents, Talbot succeeded in systematically raising the value of his invention. It is well-known how he gradually took over Herschel's sodium thiosulphate process, the use of gallic acid in developing (originally Reade's idea!), and the employment of albumin on glass, which Niepce de Saint-Victor had already demonstrated to the Academy. It is hard to understand how such a first-rate scientific inventor could so blatantly and unashamedly profit from the inventions of his rivals. His accusation against Blanquart-Evrard's "glaring act of scientific piracy" could just as well have been applied to himself.

His colleagues in the Royal Society held their tongues, and some of them even supported his calculated protests; artistic circles, however, criticized the relentlessness of his attitude and behavior toward even the most harmless of photographers. Groups of photographers, while fully recognizing the value of his contributions to the medium, pleaded with him to mitigate his rebelliousness and withdraw his demands. The instructions which Talbot gave to his representative are characteristic of his unyielding attitude: "Patents for taking portraits (only). In London: 200 guineas per year. The portraits not to be sold under one guinea; the copies not under five shillings. Not more than two cameras to be in use at the same time. Not to have more than one establishment for taking portraits. In the

country, for an *exclusive* license, for every region with 10,000 inhabitants; 100 guineas down, or else 20 guineas per year. The portraits not to be sold under one guinea each. For taking objects or views a separate license is required; the license not restricted to any particular place: 50 guineas per year, together with 25 percent on the selling price of the pictures. The pictures not to be sold under 5 shillings each. The negatives must be retained. One-half year is to be paid in advance on the above licenses. The above licenses to be terminable at the pleasure of the licensee, giving one-half year's notice of intention to terminate."

Talbot's bitterness had led him far from his original goal of achieving preeminence in his work. He was no longer interested in defending a cause, but in fighting for his commercial interests. This became manifest when he called in the bailiffs to close the studio of the unfortunate Thomas Sims because of his inability to pay Talbot the 350 pounds for his license—a license which, incidentally, concerned the use of the collodion process which was first discovered by Frederick Scott Archer. Talbot also prosecuted a number of other debtors, until finally a French-Canadian photographer who had his establishment in London had the courage to defend his rights. He collected signatures and, with the support of the Royal Society, brought Talbot before a court of law which pronounced him guilty of unlawful conduct.

Neither Talbot's genius nor the authenticity of his invention of the calotype were ever in doubt; but his right to monopolize all forms of employment and the modifications of other inventors came under heavy fire. And thus English photography attained its freedom in 1855.

Prophesies

"This remarkable phenomenon, of whatever value it may turn out in its application to the arts, will at least be accepted as a new proof of the value of the inductive methods of modern science. These methods—by making note of the occurrence of unusual circumstances which may manifest themselves in only a small degree and by following up with experiments and varying the conditions of these experiments, until the true law of nature which they express is apprehended—finally result in consequences altogether unexpected, remote from usual experience, and contrary to almost universal belief." This admirable definition of the experimental process in scientific thinking appeared in Talbot's "Account" which he read to the Royal Society on January 31, 1839. It reveals the undoubted quality of greatness inherent in Talbot's character which existed side by side with the small-mindedness already mentioned. It is therefore important to study the manuscripts left by Talbot in order to gain a clear picture of the range of his intellect, the discipline of his methods of research, and his ever-alert intuition. The Science Museum in London possesses handwritten manuscripts by Talbot concerning his work in the laboratory which are as yet unpublished. We are grateful to Dr. D. B. Thomas, Curator of The Science Museum, London, for allowing us to quote certain important passages from these manuscripts. For the most part, they contain notes, comments, observations, and research projects, and they reveal both Talbot the experimenter and Talbot the visionary. And now, over a hundred years after they were written, there is no doubt that most of his hypotheses have been proved correct.

Talbot predicted the advent of infrared photography in *The Pencil of Nature*. In addition, he sketched the possibility of the future reproduction of documents: "A glass plate covered with varnish and strongly electrified, pressed on the Daguerreotype plate, to take up the mercury powder. . . ."

He also predicted the use of photography and galvanic material in the printing process: "If a copper plate with a silver design upon it (or merely a design in resin) were made part of a galvanic series, perhaps the fresh copper deposited only on the copper plate would give *relief* to those uncovered parts, and thus furnish a substitute for woodblocks. . . ." (February 1839.)

He was also interested in macrophotography and suggested the use of an "additional lens on camera, of shorter focus, for copying near objects composed of two plan convexes which may be separated or reversed." With regard to the artistic side of the medium, he was ahead of his time and as advanced in his thinking as certain contemporary photographers, for example Christian Schad (February 18, 1839): "Make picture of kaleidoscope."

The references to the possibility of realizing certain ideas which he noted briefly in telegraphic style also have their merit if we consider when they were written: "A film of yellow liquid placed between a lens and a pane of glass would give a graduated shadow in concentric circles"; "nine lenses, grouped in rows of three, each of three inches in focus and diameter, set in a frame"; "print a woodcut with mur-tin on paper, heat it strongly and it turns out very black; write with the same, and varnish the paper with mastic to make it transparent. Copies of handwriting might be multiplied"; "telescope pictures; solar microscoped: bend paper into a cylindrical form," etc.

One thing is certain: Talbot was an outstanding scholar and thinker, even if scientific circles are reserved in crediting any one inventor with originality and priority. But is it really necessary to establish who was the true founder of photography? We are inclined to agree with Gernsheim that it is Niepce who deserves the title of the first inventor. Talbot, however, is closer to us, for it was he who developed the negative-positive process which is still valid today. His work continues to fascinate us, and time has confirmed the value of his discoveries and inventions.

Bibliographical Notes

Serious discussions of Talbot's work are few and fragmentary. The English photographer and historian, Harold White, suspended publication of the treasures of Lacock Abbey for many years with the intention of writing the long-awaited monograph on Talbot's life and work. He did not achieve his aim, however, and at present, Eugen Ostroff, Curator of the Photographic Department of the Smithsonian Institution in Washington, is occupied with the preparation of a complete catalog of the existing works of Talbot—a publication which is expected to form the basis for all future treatises on the English photographer. "Talbot's Earliest Extant Prints, June 20, 1835, Rediscovered" (*Photographic Science and Engineering*; Vol. 10, No. 6, November/December 1966, pp. 350–354), and "Early Fox Talbot Photographs and Restoration by Neutron Irradiation" (*The Journal of Photographic Science*; Vol. 13, 1965, pp. 213–227) are two discussions by Eugen Ostroff. Firsthand details on Talbot's photo-mechanical work by the same author can be found in *Etching, Engraving and Photography: History of Photomechanical Reproduction* and in *The Journal of Photographic Science*, Vol. 17, 1969, pp. 65–80 and 101–115.

Until more comprehensive studies are available, the small book entitled *William Henry Fox Talbot, Father of Modern Photography* by Arthur H. Booth, published in the series "Creators of the Modern World" by Arthur Barker Ltd., London, 1964, is worthy of our attention.

The latest edition of *The History of Photography* by Helmut and Alison Gernsheim (Thames and Hudson, 1969, 600 pages, 390 illustrations) contains numerous references to Talbot and his contemporaries, with comprehensive text and footnotes. The most clear-sighted studies on Talbot are incontestably those by Beaumont Newhall, mentioned in chronological order: *Image* (No. 2, June 1959, George Eastman House, Rochester), a publication largely dedicated to "the prophetic pioneer" Talbot, his life, and his work *The Pencil of Nature* (pp. 58–105); *Latent Image: the Discovery of Photography* (Doubleday and Co., Anchor Books, New York 1967); and the hitherto most comprehensive study on the work of the pioneers—above all Niepce, Daguerre, and Talbot— *William Henry Fox Talbot: The Pencil of Nature*, new introduction by Beaumont Newhall (Da Capo Press, New York 1969), an impressive book with an instructive introduction and a comprehensive bibliography (although the reproduction of the pictures is unfortunately unsatisfactory). Finally, worthy of mention is the excellent study by D. B. Thomas, a monograph of the Science Museum: *The First Negatives, and Account of the Discovery and Early Use of the Negative-Positive Photographic Process* (London 1964), a summary with previously unpublished text and pictures. The fine catalog of *The Science Museum Photography Collection*, published by the Museum's Curator, D. B. Thomas, also contains some important references to Talbot.

These bibliographical notes would appear to require the expression of the hope that a critical work on Talbot's laboratory journals will not be long in appearing (the journals are in the possession of the Science Museum in London and contain an abundance of important information). The Talbot-Biot correspondence is also valuable for a comprehensive publication— the greater part of which is still in existence; it would provide information facilitating a more precise evaluation of the progress made by Daguerre and Talbot, as seen through the eyes of these two scientists who participated in the very early experiments in the photographic medium. This also would provide a criterion of the value ascribed to the realization and publication of the new art in scientific circles.

Talbot's First Experiments

Photo captions may be found on page 95

150694

GERTRUDE KISTLER MEMORIAL LIBRARY
ROSEMONT COLLEGE
ROSEMONT, PENNSYLVANIA 19010

1

2

3

Photogenic Drawings

4

5

6

7

9

11

12

The Idea of the Negative

are led to look for the phænomena of mixed plates in minerals, such as *sulphate of lime* and *mica*, where a plate of two different thicknesses can be easily obtained. I have accordingly discovered the phænomena of mixed plates distinctly exhibited in sulphate of lime and mica.

A more splendid exhibition of these colours is seen when a stratum of cavities of extreme thinness occurs in sulphate of lime. I have observed such strata repeatedly in the gypsum from Mont-martre; but they are most beautiful when the stratum has a circular form. In this case the cavities are exceedingly thin at the circumference of the circle, and gradually increase in depth towards the centre, so that we have a series of edges increasing in thickness towards a centre; the very reverse of a mixed plate, such as a film of albumen pressed between two convex surfaces. The system of rings is therefore also reversed, the highest order of colours being in the centre, while the lowest are at the circumference of the circular stratum. In many strata of cavities, such as the one which I have engraven in my paper on the new fluids in minerals*, the cavities are too deep to give the colours of mixed plates.

Another example of the colours of mixed plates in natural bodies occurs in specimens of mica, through which titanium is disseminated in beautiful flat dendritic crystals of various degrees of opacity and transparency. In these specimens the titanium is often disseminated in grains, forming an irregular surface. The edges of these grains, by retarding the light which they transmit, produce the direct and complementary colours of mixed plates in the most perfect manner, the tints passing through two orders of colours as the grains of titanium increase in size towards the interior of the irregular patch. I have observed another example of these colours in the deep cavities of topaz, from which the fluids have either escaped, leaving one or both of the surfaces covered with minute particles of transparent matter, or in which the fluids have suffered induration.

Allerly by Melrose, Oct. 18, 1837.

XXXVII. *Some Account of the Art of Photogenic Drawing.*
By H. F. Talbot, *Esq.,* F.R.S.†

§ 1.

IN the spring of 1834 I began to put in practice a method which I had devised some time previously, for employing

* Edinburgh Transactions, vol. x. plate ii. fig. 33.
† Read before the Royal Society on the 31st of January, and communicated by the Author.

14

15

16

The First Calotypes

17

18

19

20

21

22

Portraits and Group Photographs

The Studio in Reading

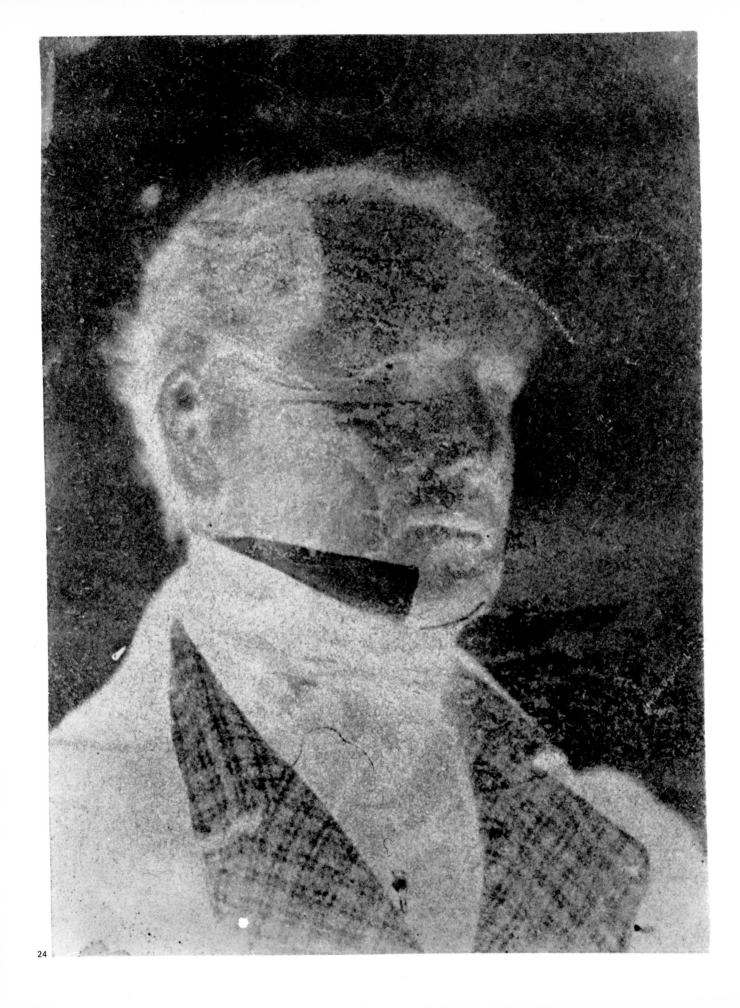

24

25

29

30

32

33

34

35

36

37

The Art of the Calotype

BY ROYAL LETTERS PATENT.

IODISED PAPER,

FOR MAKING

SUN PICTURES.

PREPARED BY

N. HENNEMAN, RUSSELL TERRACE, READING.

Five Sheets, 3s.; or, to Licensees, 2s. 6d.

NOTICE TO PURCHASERS.

This Paper is prepared for the convenience of *Amateurs*, who *engage* to use the same *bonâ fide for purposes of amusement only.*

Persons wishing to make a commercial or professional use of the Art can take out a License from the Patentee.

All applications for Licenses to be addressed to Mr. HENNEMAN, *Reading.*

*Received of H. F. Talbot Esq. 2.6.0, Tables
I wish the above is one   Laycock abbey Decr 11th 46
                                                 N. Henneman*

40

42

43

44

45

46

48

The Pencil of Nature
Sun Pictures in Scotland

Notice to the Reader.

————◆————

The plates of the present work are impressed by the agency of Light alone, without any aid whatever from the artist's pencil.   They are the sun-pictures themselves, and not, as some persons have imagined, engravings in imitation.

The
Pencil of Nature
by
H. Fox Talbot
F.R.S.

LONGMAN, BROWN, GREEN AND LONGMANS.

LONDON, 1844.

54

55

Scientific Application

Subscribers
to the Talbotype Sun Pictures in Scotland
1845

Her Majesty the Queen
The Queen Dowager
the Duke of Devonshire
Lord Dudley Stuart _ __2 copies
Earl of Auckland
Lord Seymour
Sir William Gallwey
Duchess of St Albans
Earl of Haddington
Sir Robert Throckmorton
Earl of Mount Edgcumbe
Honble Mrs Damer

60

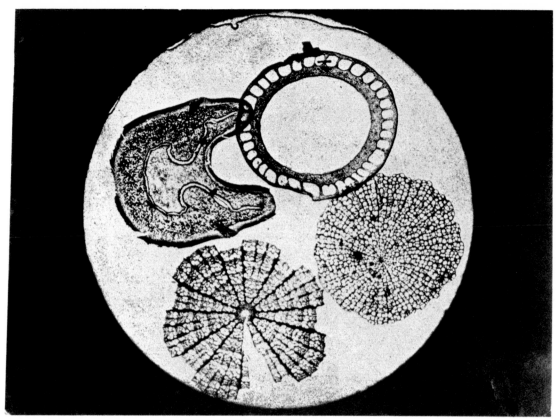

61

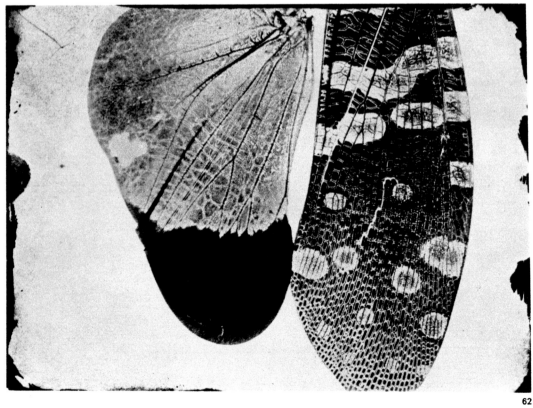

62

The date of this Tablet, according to Chevr. Bunsen, falls between 1397 and 1387 B.C.

63

The Photomechanical Process

67

the Duke of Edinburgh.　　　　aged 18

from a photograph made in that City.

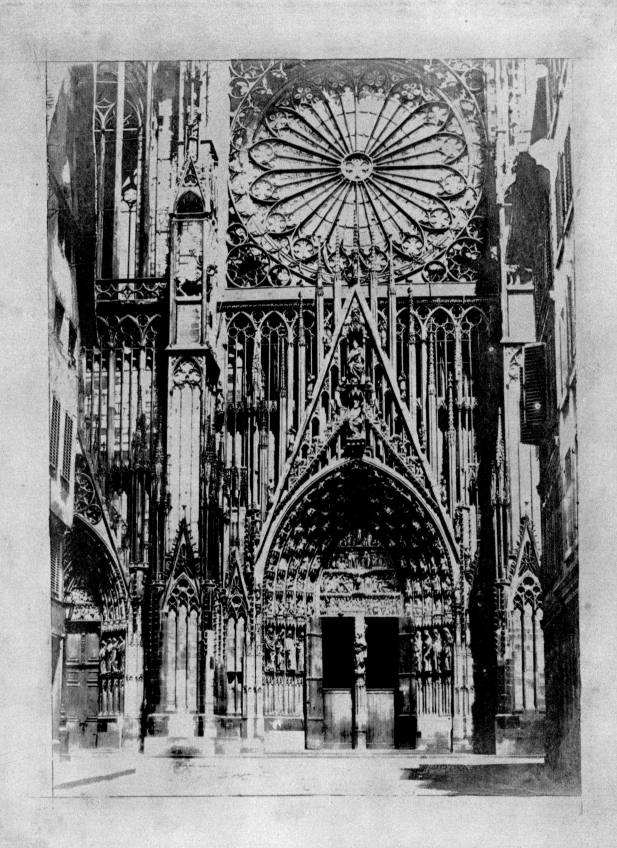

Captions

1 William H. Fox Talbot (1800–1877). "Carte de visite" by John Moffat of Edinburgh, May 1866. Almost double-sized enlargement.

2 View of Griante. Taken by Talbot with a *camera obscura* in a light room in 1833.

3 *Camera obscura* used by Talbot.

4 Photogenic drawing. The watermark of the handwritten original is dated 1811; the reproduction is in black on sensitized paper, but its watermark (from 183?) is in white.

5 Photogenic drawing: fragment of fabric (ca. 1835).

6 Photogenic drawing: moss and lace (between 1835 and 1839).

7 Photogenic drawing (1839).

8 Photogenic drawing (between 1839 and 1842).

9 Photogenic drawing (between 1839 and 1842).

10/11 Talbot's printing establishment in Reading. These two pictures give an insight into Talbot's range of work: reproductions of pictures or etchings and sculptures; portraiture; the printing of pictures in sunlight. Also recognizable are the clocks by the cameras, the headrest behind the seated model, the focal length meter for the correct focusing of the camera (right), and the "glass-house" for overcast days.

12 Group of three calotype cameras used by Talbot between 1840 and 1842.

13 Positive and negative prints on waxed paper; an issue of the magazine in which the memorandum to the Royal Society appeared (January 31, 1839).

14 Laokoon; reproduction of an antique group; negative print.

15 Idem. (Positive print.)

16 A glass window in Lacock Abbey. The oldest known negative (August 1835). The original is violet-toned.

17 The terrace at Lacock Abbey (1835). "The outline of the roof and of the chimneys, etc. against the sky was marked enough; but the details of the architecture were feeble, and the parts in shade were left either blank or nearly so."

18 Lacock Abbey; negative print, dated July 1842.

19 Lacock Abbey; positive print (1842?).

20 Lacock Abbey; negative print, dated September 17, 1841 by Talbot.

21 The library at Lacock Abbey; negative print (ca. 1844).

22 "Breakfast." Calotype (ca. 1841).

23 Group; positive print, dated April 8, 1842 by Talbot.

24 Enlargement. The original is 61 mm. × 84 mm. in size (marked "G.M." in Talbot's handwriting).

25 "The Handshake." Enlargement of a calotype negative. The original measured 118 mm.× 123 mm. (dated April 8, 1842 by Talbot).

26 Portrait of Sir David Brewster (1841?). "...I was one of the first, if not the first, to suggest that the expression 'calotype' be changed to Talbotype...."

27 Early calotype; man seated on sofa; positive print (October 1841).

28 Group; positive print (between 1842 and 1844).

29 "Lady at the Harp." Miss Horatia Fielding, Talbot's half-sister; calotype (ca. 1842).

30 Two figures in the garden of Lacock Abbey (between 1842 and 1844).

31 Group in the Lacock Abbey cloister (ca. 1844).

32 On the terrace at Bowood (ca. 1844).

33 Child in the Lacock Abbey cloister. Possibly Ela, Talbot's elder daughter; negative dated 1844.

34 Two children in the Lacock Abbey cloister. Possibly Rosamund and Ela, Talbot's two elder daughters; dated 1844.

35 The keeper at Lacock Abbey (ca. 1844).

36 "The Chess Players." Calotype (ca. 1843).

37 Portrait of a man (ca. 1843); possibly taken with the help of Henry Collen.

38 Label advertising iodized paper for making "sun pictures" (by Henneman, Talbot's assistant, 1846).

39 "The Old Bridge." Negative, dated July 30, 1842 by Talbot.

40 Reproduction by means of a calotype from an early lithographic illustration from the Senefelder Studio in Munich (ca. 1844).

41 Talbot's carriage in Lacock Abbey (ca. 1842).

42 "Tree in Winter." Calotype. Numerous similar prints were used as illustrations for *The Art Union* in 1840.

43 Notre-Dame cathedral, Paris. Calotype (1843), probably the oldest photograph of this building.

44 "L'Hôtel Canterbury"; negative (1843).

45/46 Negative calotype; view from the window of Talbot's flat in the Rue de la Paix in Paris (1843).

47 "Seashore Landscape." Negative (1843 or 1844).

48 "Sailing Ships at Low Tide." Calotype (ca. 1845).

49 "Suspension Bridge." Negative (ca. 1846).

50 The Lacock Abbey cloister (1844).

51 Notice to the reader in *The Pencil of Nature* and *Sun Pictures in Scotland* volumes. ("Notice to the Reader. The plates of the present work are impressed by the agency of Light alone, without any aid whatever from the artist's pencil. They are the sun-pictures themselves, and not, as some persons have imagined, engravings in imitation.")

52 Cover of one of *The Pencil of Nature* volumes.

53 "The Open Door." Calotype from *The Pencil of Nature*, plate VI.

54 Calotype from *The Pencil of Nature*, still life of Talbot's library. The titles reveal the wide range of his interests: *Manners and Customs of the Ancient Egyptians*, *Philological Essays*, *Miscellanies of Science*, Lanzi's *Botanische Schriften*, and *The Philosophical Magazine*.

55 View of the Paris boulevards taken from the first floor of the Hôtel de Louvais on the corner of the Rue de la Paix.

56 "The Ladder," from *The Pencil of Nature*, plate XIV.

57 "Fruit," from *The Pencil of Nature*, plate XXIV.

58 *Sun Pictures in Scotland*. The first page of the subscribers' list.

59 A solar microscope used by Talbot.

60 "Sea Shell." Negative calotype.

61 Calotype; photomicrograph taken with a solar microscope (1841).

62 Calotype photomicrograph. Butterflies' wings, enlarged with the aid of a solar microscope (1841).

63 Illustration for *The Talbotype Applied to Hieroglyphics* (1847).

64 "Seeds." Enlargement of a detail of 57 mm. × 78 mm.

65/66 Botanical objects; photoglyptic gravure. The structural details are clearly recognizable.

67 Reproduction of an etching; photoglyptic gravure.

68 The Duke of Edinburgh at the age of eighteen. (Talbot's comment: "From a photograph made in that city.")

69 Strasbourg cathedral; photoglyptic gravure. The fine quality of the resin dust allowed the reproduction of the finest details.

Front cover: Group; positive calotype (between 1842 and 1844).
Back cover: "Suspension Bridge." Negative (ca. 1846).

Index

ROMEO E. MARTINEZ

As editor of this series, Romeo E. Martinez crowns an almost forty-year career as journalist and picture director.

Martinez was chief of the illustration department with the magazines *Vu* and *Excelsior* in Paris and is a member of the *Conseil en illustrations de la "Grande Encyclopédie française."*

His ten years as editor-in-chief of the monthly magazine *Camera* in Lucerne contributed greatly to the success of this journal. He has been responsible for the organization of the biennial of photography in Venice.

ANDRÉ JAMMES

André Jammes is a writer, bookseller, collector, and owner of one of the finest collections of old photographs in Europe. He has published numerous articles, mainly on the history of typography and the development of printing techniques. In 1963 he received the *Prix Nadar* for his book on Charles Nègres. He has initiated numerous exhibitions, including that devoted to "Early French Photography" which was first shown in Philadelphia in 1969 and has since traveled to New York, Pasadena, St. Louis, Ottawa, and Boston. André Jammes is a member of the *Conseil de la Société française de photographie.*

ACKNOWLEDGMENTS

Most of the photographs published in this work originate from the André Jammes Collection. Illustrations 1, 2, 3, 10, 11, 12, 16, 22, 27, 29, 30, 35, 36, 38, 42, 43, 48, 53, 54, 58, 59, 60, 61, 62, and 63 are the property of the Science Museum, London, to whom we should like to express our sincere thanks for the permission to reproduce these pictures.

REYNOLDS KISTLER MEMORIAL LIBRARY
ROSEMONT COLLEGE
ROSEMONT, PENNSYLVANIA 19010

Rosemont College Library
TR651 .T3413   KISTLER
Talbot, William Hen/William H. Fox Talbo

3 1251 00018 4673

DATE DUE   TR   T3413
              65I   I50694

DEMCO 25-370